THE
HANDBOOK OF AI AND ML

A Comprehensive handbook on recent trends

Preface

Welcome to "The Handbook to AI and ML," an exploration into the captivating world of Artificial Intelligence (AI) and Machine Learning (ML). In the ever-evolving landscape of technology, AI and ML stand as pillars of innovation, reshaping industries, solving complex problems, and illuminating the path toward a smarter, data-driven future.

This handbook seeks to be your compass through the vast terrain of AI and ML, whether you're a curious beginner or a seasoned professional. Drawing from a wealth of experience and knowledge, this book is designed to provide a clear and comprehensive understanding of these transformative fields.

Our journey begins with fundamental concepts, unraveling the essence of machine learning algorithms and demystifying neural networks. With each chapter, we delve deeper into the intricacies of AI, exploring topics such as natural language understanding, generative adversarial networks (GANs), and the ever-intriguing quantum computing.

As you navigate through these pages, you'll not only grasp the theoretical foundations but also witness how these theories are translated into practical applications. Discover how AI is reshaping industries, from healthcare and finance to robotics and autonomous agents, and learn how you can apply AI and ML solutions in your own domain.

But our exploration doesn't stop at mere technical knowledge. We also dive into ethical considerations, addressing the responsibilities that come with wielding AI's power. With great potential comes great responsibility, and it's crucial to uphold ethical standards, ensure privacy, and mitigate bias in the age of AI.

Each chapter is carefully crafted to provide you with the insights, examples, and tools you need to thrive in the world of AI and ML. Whether you're interested in building a strong foundation, staying updated with the latest advancements, or contributing to groundbreaking research, this handbook is your trusty companion.

As you turn the pages, you'll gain not just knowledge but a profound understanding of the profound impact AI and ML have on our lives. You'll become part of a community of innovators, creators, and problem solvers who are driving the future of artificial intelligence.

So, without further ado, let's embark on this journey through "The Handbook to AI and ML." Let's explore, learn, innovate, and together, shape the future of technology.

Welcome aboard.

Table of Contents

Chapter 1: Introduction to Artificial Intelligence and Machine Learning

1.1 What is Artificial Intelligence?

Artificial Intelligence, often abbreviated as AI, is a field of computer science that aims to create machines and software that can perform tasks that typically require human intelligence. These tasks include understanding natural language, recognizing patterns, making decisions, and learning from experience.

1.2 The Birth of AI

The concept of AI has its roots in ancient history, with early ideas about automating human-like tasks. However, modern AI as we know it began to take shape in the mid-20th century, with the development of electronic computers and the work of pioneers like Alan Turing and John McCarthy.

1.3 Machine Learning: A Subset of AI

Machine Learning (ML) is a subfield of AI that focuses on developing algorithms and models that allow computers to learn from data and make predictions or decisions without being explicitly programmed. ML has gained immense popularity in recent years due to its wide range of applications.

1.4 The Importance of AI and ML

AI and ML have already revolutionized various industries, including healthcare, finance, and transportation. They have the potential to drive innovation, automate tasks, and improve decision-making across multiple domains.

1.5 Applications of AI and ML

1.5.1 Natural Language Processing (NLP)

NLP is a branch of AI that deals with the interaction between humans and computers through natural language. It enables machines to understand, interpret, and generate human language.

1.5.2 Computer Vision

Computer Vision involves teaching computers to interpret and understand visual information from the world, such as images and videos. It's essential for applications like image recognition and autonomous vehicles.

1.5.3 Recommender Systems
Recommender systems use ML algorithms to provide personalized recommendations to s, such as movie recommendations on streaming platforms or product recommendations on e-commerce websites.

1.5.4 Healthcare
AI and ML are transforming healthcare by assisting in diagnosis, drug discovery, and treatment planning. They can analyze medical images, predict disease outbreaks, and improve patient outcomes.

1.6 The Structure of This Handbook
This handbook is designed to provide a comprehensive overview of AI and ML concepts, algorithms, and practical applications. Each chapter will delve into specific topics and provide code examples in Python where applicable.

Chapter 2: Foundations of Machine Learning

2.1 What is Machine Learning?

Machine Learning is a subset of artificial intelligence that focuses on developing algorithms and models that allow computers to learn from data and make predictions or decisions without being explicitly programmed. It's based on the idea that machines can improve their performance on a task with experience.

2.2 Types of Machine Learning

2.2.1 Supervised Learning

In supervised learning, the algorithm is trained on a labeled dataset, where each data point is associated with a target output. The goal is to learn a mapping from input to output that can be used to make predictions on new, unseen data.

2.2.2 Unsupervised Learning

Unsupervised learning involves training on unlabeled data, with the objective of discovering hidden patterns or structures within the data. Common techniques include clustering and dimensionality reduction.

2.2.3 Reinforcement Learning

Reinforcement learning is about training agents to make sequences of decisions to maximize a reward. It's often used in applications like game playing, robotics, and autonomous systems.

2.3 Machine Learning Workflow

The typical machine learning workflow consists of several key steps:

- Data Collection: Gathering and preparing the data for training and evaluation.
- Data Preprocessing: Cleaning, transforming, and scaling the data to make it suitable for learning algorithms.
- Model Selection: Choosing an appropriate machine learning algorithm or model.
- Training: Using the training data to teach the model to make predictions.
- Evaluation: Assessing the model's performance on unseen data.
- Deployment: Integrating the trained model into a real-world application.

2.4 Algorithms in Machine Learning

2.4.1 Linear Regression

Linear regression is a supervised learning algorithm used for predicting a continuous output variable based on one or more input features. It assumes a linear relationship between the inputs and the target.

2.4.2 Decision Trees

Decision trees are versatile algorithms that can be used for both classification and regression tasks. They partition the data into subsets based on feature values, making decisions at each node.

2.4.3 Neural Networks

Neural networks, inspired by the human brain, consist of interconnected nodes (neurons) organized into layers. They excel at tasks like image recognition and natural language processing.

2.4.4 Support Vector Machines (SVM)

SVMs are powerful algorithms for both classification and regression. They aim to find the hyperplane that best separates data points of different classes while maximizing the margin.

2.5 Python for Machine Learning

Python is the go-to programming language for machine learning due to its simplicity and a rich ecosystem of libraries. In this handbook, we'll use Python for coding examples to illustrate various ML concepts.

2.5.1 Installing Python and Libraries

To get started, make sure you have Python installed on your system. You can then use popular libraries like NumPy, pandas, and scikit-learn for data manipulation and machine learning tasks.

2.5.2 Your First Machine Learning Model in Python

Let's create a simple Python script that uses scikit-learn to build a linear regression model. This example will serve as a foundation for more complex ML models discussed in later chapters.

In this script, we import necessary libraries, define some sample data, create a linear regression model, and make predictions.

```python
import numpy as np
from sklearn.linear_model import LinearRegression


# Sample data
X = np.array([1, 2, 3, 4, 5]).reshape(-1, 1)
y = np.array([2, 4, 5, 4, 5])


# Create and train the model
model = LinearRegression()
model.fit(X, y)


# Make predictions
predictions = model.predict([[6]])
print("Predicted value for 6:", predictions[0])
```

This chapter has laid the foundation for understanding machine learning concepts and using Python for implementing them. In the following chapters, we will delve deeper into specific machine learning techniques and their applications.

Chapter 3: Data Preprocessing and Feature Engineering

3.1 The Importance of Data Preprocessing

Data preprocessing is a crucial step in machine learning because the quality of your data directly impacts the performance of your models. It involves cleaning, transforming, and preparing data for training and analysis.

3.2 Data Cleaning

Data cleaning is the process of identifying and correcting errors, inconsistencies, and missing values in your dataset. Common tasks include:

- Removing duplicate records.
- Handling missing values by imputation or deletion.
- Correcting inconsistent data formats.

3.3 Data Transformation

Data transformation involves changing the format or scale of your data to make it suitable for machine learning algorithms. Common techniques include:

- Scaling features to have a consistent range.
- Encoding categorical variables into numerical values.
- Normalizing data to have a standard distribution.

3.4 Feature Engineering

Feature engineering is the process of creating new features from existing ones or selecting the most relevant features for your machine learning model. Effective feature engineering can significantly improve model performance.

3.5 Exploratory Data Analysis (EDA)

EDA is a critical part of data preprocessing. It involves visualizing and analyzing data to gain insights and identify patterns. Popular Python libraries like Matplotlib and Seaborn are often used for EDA.

3.6 Dimensionality Reduction

In cases where the dataset has a high number of features, dimensionality reduction techniques like Principal Component Analysis (PCA) can help reduce the number of dimensions while preserving as much information as possible.

3.7 Handling Imbalanced Data

Imbalanced datasets occur when one class of data significantly outweighs the other(s). Handling such datasets requires techniques like oversampling, undersampling, or using specialized algorithms designed for imbalanced data.

3.8 Data Preprocessing in Python

Let's explore some common data preprocessing tasks using Python and the Pandas library. We'll focus on handling missing values and encoding categorical variables.

```python
import pandas as pd

from sklearn.preprocessing import LabelEncoder


# Sample dataset

data = pd.DataFrame({'Gender': ['Male', 'Female', 'Male',
'Female', 'Male'],

                     'Age': [25, 30, None, 28, 35],

                     'Salary': [50000, 60000, 55000, None,
70000]})


# Handling missing values

data['Age'].fillna(data['Age'].median(), inplace=True)

data['Salary'].fillna(data['Salary'].mean(), inplace=True)


# Encoding categorical variables

label_encoder = LabelEncoder()

data['Gender'] = label_encoder.fit_transform(data['Gender'])


print(data)
```

In this example, we replace missing values with the median for 'Age' and the mean for 'Salary,' and we encode the 'Gender' column into numerical values.

Data preprocessing is a critical skill for any machine learning practitioner, as it ensures that your models are trained on clean and relevant data. In the subsequent chapters, we'll dive deeper into various machine learning algorithms and techniques for solving real-world problems.

Chapter 4: Supervised Learning Algorithms

4.1 Supervised Learning Recap

Supervised learning is a type of machine learning where the algorithm learns from labeled training data to make predictions or decisions. In this chapter, we'll explore some of the most commonly used supervised learning algorithms.

4.2 Linear Regression

Linear regression is a simple but powerful algorithm for regression tasks. It models the relationship between the input variables and the continuous target variable as a linear equation. The goal is to find the best-fit line that minimizes the sum of squared errors.

4.3 Logistic Regression

Logistic regression is used for binary classification tasks. It models the probability that a given input belongs to one of the two classes. Despite the name, logistic regression is a classification algorithm.

4.4 Decision Trees

Decision trees are versatile algorithms for both classification and regression. They work by recursively partitioning the data into subsets based on feature values. Decision trees are easy to interpret and can handle both categorical and numerical data.

4.5 Random Forest

Random Forest is an ensemble learning method that combines multiple decision trees to improve accuracy and reduce overfitting. It's a powerful algorithm for both classification and regression tasks.

4.6 Support Vector Machines (SVM)

Support Vector Machines are popular for binary classification tasks. They aim to find the hyperplane that best separates data points of different classes while maximizing the margin between them.

4.7 k-Nearest Neighbors (k-NN)

k-NN is a simple but effective algorithm for classification and regression. It makes predictions based on the majority class among the k-nearest data points in the feature space.

4.8 Naive Bayes

Naive Bayes is a probabilistic algorithm used for classification tasks, particularly in text classification and spam detection. It's based on Bayes' theorem and assumes that features are independent.

4.9 Gradient Boosting

Gradient boosting is an ensemble learning technique that combines weak learners (usually decision trees) into a strong learner. Popular implementations include XGBoost and LightGBM.

4.10 Neural Networks

Neural networks, inspired by the human brain, consist of interconnected nodes organized into layers. They can handle complex tasks such as image recognition, natural language processing, and more. Deep learning, a subset of neural networks, involves training deep architectures with many layers.

4.11 Choosing the Right Algorithm

Selecting the appropriate algorithm for your machine learning task is essential. Factors to consider include the nature of the problem (classification or regression), the size and quality of the dataset, and computational resources.

4.12 Python Implementation

In this section, we'll provide Python code examples for implementing some of the discussed supervised learning algorithms. Let's look at an example for logistic regression using scikit-learn.

```python
from sklearn.datasets import load_iris
from sklearn.model_selection import train_test_split
from sklearn.linear_model import LogisticRegression
from sklearn.metrics import accuracy_score


# Load the Iris dataset
data = load_iris()
X = data.data
y = data.target


# Split the dataset into training and testing sets
X_train, X_test, y_train, y_test = train_test_split(X, y,
test_size=0.2, random_state=42)


# Create and train the logistic regression model
model = LogisticRegression()
model.fit(X_train, y_train)


# Make predictions
y_pred = model.predict(X_test)


# Calculate accuracy
accuracy = accuracy_score(y_test, y_pred)
print("Accuracy:", accuracy)
```

This code demonstrates how to load a dataset, split it into training and testing sets, create a logistic regression model, and evaluate its accuracy.

Chapter 5: Unsupervised Learning Algorithms

5.1 Unsupervised Learning Overview

Unsupervised learning is a category of machine learning where the algorithm learns patterns, structures, or representations from unlabeled data. In this chapter, we'll explore some of the most widely used unsupervised learning algorithms.

5.2 Clustering

Clustering is a common unsupervised learning task that involves grouping similar data points together. Some popular clustering algorithms include:

K-Means Clustering: Divides data into k clusters based on similarity.

Hierarchical Clustering: Builds a tree-like structure of clusters.

DBSCAN (Density-Based Spatial Clustering of Applications with Noise): Identifies clusters of arbitrary shapes.

5.3 Principal Component Analysis (PCA)

PCA is a dimensionality reduction technique used for feature selection and data visualization. It transforms high-dimensional data into a lower-dimensional representation while preserving as much variance as possible.

5.4 Independent Component Analysis (ICA)

ICA is another dimensionality reduction technique that aims to find independent components in the data. It's useful for source separation tasks, such as separating mixed audio signals.

5.5 Association Rule Learning

Association rule learning discovers interesting relationships or patterns in transactional data. A well-known algorithm in this category is Apriori, which finds frequent itemsets in a dataset.

5.6 Anomaly Detection

Anomaly detection identifies data points that deviate significantly from the norm. One-class SVM and Isolation Forest are commonly used for this purpose.

5.7 Recommender Systems

Recommender systems, while often associated with supervised learning, can also be implemented using unsupervised techniques. Collaborative filtering and matrix factorization are examples of such approaches.

5.8 Autoencoders

Autoencoders are neural networks used for unsupervised feature learning and data compression. They consist of an encoder that maps input data to a lower-dimensional representation and a decoder that reconstructs the data from that representation.

5.9 Generative Adversarial Networks (GANs)

GANs are a class of unsupervised learning algorithms used for generating synthetic data that closely resembles real data. They consist of two neural networks, a generator, and a discriminator, which compete against each other in a training process.

```python
import numpy as np

from sklearn.decomposition import PCA


# Sample data

X = np.random.rand(100, 5)  # 100 samples with 5 features


# Create a PCA instance

pca = PCA(n_components=2)


# Fit and transform the data

X_pca = pca.fit_transform(X)


print("Original shape:", X.shape)

print("Reduced shape:", X_pca.shape)
```

5.10 Dimensionality Reduction in Practice

Let's explore dimensionality reduction using PCA as an example in Python:

In this example, we use PCA to reduce the dimensionality of random data from 5 features to 2 features.

Unsupervised learning plays a vital role in data exploration, feature extraction, and data compression. Understanding these algorithms will enhance your ability to uncover hidden patterns and insights in your data.

In the upcoming chapters, we'll delve deeper into the practical aspects of using unsupervised learning techniques for various applications.

Chapter 6: Reinforcement Learning

6.1 Introduction to Reinforcement Learning

Reinforcement Learning (RL) is a type of machine learning where an agent learns to make a sequence of decisions by interacting with an environment. The agent's goal is to maximize a cumulative reward signal.

6.2 Key Components of RL

RL involves several key components:

- Agent: The learner or decision-maker.
- Environment: The external system with which the agent interacts.
- State (s): A representation of the environment at a particular time.
- Action (a): The choices made by the agent to interact with the environment.
- Reward (r): A scalar feedback signal indicating the immediate desirability of the agent's action.
- Policy (π): A strategy that the agent uses to determine its actions.

6.3 Markov Decision Processes (MDPs)

MDPs are a mathematical framework used to model RL problems. They consist of a finite set of states, actions, transition probabilities, rewards, and a discount factor. MDPs provide a formal way to describe sequential decision-making problems.

6.4 Exploration vs. Exploitation

In RL, the agent faces a trade-off between exploration (trying new actions to discover their effects) and exploitation (choosing actions that are known to yield high rewards). Balancing these two aspects is a fundamental challenge in RL.

6.5 Q-Learning

Q-Learning is a popular RL algorithm used for solving problems where an agent learns an action-value function (Q-function). It iteratively updates Q-values to maximize the expected cumulative reward.

6.6 Deep Reinforcement Learning

Deep Reinforcement Learning combines RL with deep neural networks. Deep Q-Networks (DQNs) and Proximal Policy Optimization (PPO) are examples of deep RL algorithms. They excel in tasks like game playing and robotic control.

6.7 Policy Gradients

Policy Gradients is an RL approach that directly learns the policy (strategy) by maximizing expected rewards. It's suitable for problems with continuous action spaces and is used in applications like robotics and natural language processing.

6.8 Reinforcement Learning in Practice

Let's implement a simple RL example using the OpenAI Gym library, which provides a wide range of environments for RL tasks. We'll use the CartPole environment.

```python
import gym
# Create the CartPole environment
env = gym.make('CartPole-v1')
# Initialize Q-values or policy network
# (Not shown here, as it depends on the specific algorithm)
# Training loop
for episode in range(1000):
    state = env.reset()
    total_reward = 0
    while True:
        # Choose an action based on the current policy
        action = policy(state)  # Replace with your policy function
        # Take the chosen action and observe the next state and reward
        next_state, reward, done, _ = env.step(action)
        # Update the Q-values or policy network
        # (Not shown here, as it depends on the specific algorithm)
        total_reward += reward
        state = next_state
        if done:
            break
    print(f"Episode {episode + 1}: Total Reward = {total_reward}")
# Continue training or use the learned policy for decision-making
```

This code demonstrates a basic RL training loop using the CartPole environment.

Reinforcement Learning is a powerful paradigm for solving problems that involve sequential decision-making and interaction with dynamic environments. Understanding RL algorithms and their applications is crucial for tackling complex tasks in robotics, gaming, and more.

Chapter 7: Natural Language Processing

7.1 Introduction to Natural Language Processing (NLP)

Natural Language Processing is a field of artificial intelligence that focuses on the interaction between computers and human language. It encompasses a wide range of tasks, from text understanding and sentiment analysis to language generation and machine translation.

7.2 Text Preprocessing

Before applying NLP techniques, text data often requires preprocessing steps, including:

Tokenization: Splitting text into words or subword units.

Stopword Removal: Removing common words like "the," "is," and "and" that don't carry significant meaning.

Stemming and Lemmatization: Reducing words to their root form.

Lowercasing: Converting all text to lowercase for consistency.

7.3 Bag of Words (BoW) and TF-IDF

BoW and TF-IDF are two common approaches for representing text data.

Bag of Words (BoW) represents text as a vector of word frequencies.

Term Frequency-Inverse Document Frequency (TF-IDF) assigns weights to words based on their importance in a document relative to a corpus of documents.

7.4 Word Embeddings

Word embeddings are dense vector representations of words that capture semantic relationships between words. Word2Vec and GloVe are popular word embedding techniques.

7.5 Text Classification

Text classification is the task of assigning predefined categories or labels to text documents. It's used in spam detection, sentiment analysis, and topic categorization. Machine learning algorithms like Naive Bayes and Support Vector Machines are commonly used for text classification.

7.6 Named Entity Recognition (NER)

NER is the process of identifying and classifying named entities such as names of people, organizations, locations, and dates in text. It's crucial for information extraction and search engines.

7.7 Part-of-Speech Tagging (POS)

POS tagging involves assigning grammatical tags (e.g., noun, verb, adjective) to each word in a sentence. It's used for syntactic analysis and language understanding.

7.8 Sentiment Analysis

Sentiment analysis, or opinion mining, determines the sentiment (positive, negative, neutral) expressed in text. It's applied to customer reviews, social media monitoring, and market research.

7.9 Machine Translation

Machine translation aims to automatically translate text from one language to another. Google Translate and neural machine translation models like Transformer have advanced this field.

7.10 Speech Recognition and Generation

NLP extends to speech recognition, converting spoken language into text, and speech generation, converting text into spoken language. This is used in voice assistants like Siri and chatbots.

7.11 Natural Language Understanding (NLU)

NLU combines NLP techniques with machine learning to enable computers to understand the meaning and context of human language. It's a fundamental component of AI-powered applications.

7.12 Python Libraries for NLP

Python offers powerful libraries for NLP, including NLTK, spaCy, and the Hugging Face Transformers library. These libraries provide pre-trained models and tools for various NLP tasks.

7.13 Example: Sentiment Analysis with spaCy

Here's an example of sentiment analysis using spaCy:

```python
import spacy

# Load the spaCy English model

nlp = spacy.load("en_core_web_sm")

# Analyze text

text = "I loved the movie. It was fantastic!"

doc = nlp(text)

# Extract sentiment score (positive, neutral, negative)

sentiment_score = doc.sentiment.polarity

if sentiment_score > 0:

    sentiment = "positive"

elif sentiment_score < 0:

    sentiment = "negative"

else:

    sentiment = "neutral"

print(f"Sentiment:      {sentiment}      (Polarity      Score:
{sentiment_score})")
```

In this code, spaCy is used to analyze the sentiment of a text document.

Natural Language Processing is a rapidly evolving field with diverse applications. Understanding NLP techniques and tools is crucial for building intelligent systems that can understand and generate human language.

Chapter 8: Computer Vision

8.1 Introduction to Computer Vision

Computer Vision is a subfield of artificial intelligence that focuses on teaching computers to interpret and understand visual information from the world, such as images and videos. It plays a crucial role in applications like image recognition, object detection, and autonomous vehicles.

8.2 Image Representation

Images are represented as grids of pixels, with each pixel containing color information. Common color spaces include RGB (Red, Green, Blue) and grayscale.

8.3 Image Preprocessing

Before applying computer vision algorithms, images often undergo preprocessing steps, including:

Resize: Adjusting image dimensions for consistent processing.

Grayscale Conversion: Reducing color information to grayscale.

Denoising: Removing noise or unwanted artifacts.

Normalization: Scaling pixel values to a common range.

8.4 Edge Detection

Edge detection is the process of identifying boundaries in images. Techniques like the Sobel operator and Canny edge detector are used to highlight edges.

8.5 Image Segmentation

Image segmentation divides an image into meaningful regions or objects. Techniques like watershed segmentation and k-means clustering are commonly used.

8.6 Object Detection

Object detection is the task of identifying and locating objects of interest within an image. Convolutional Neural Networks (CNNs) are the foundation of modern object detection algorithms, with architectures like Faster R-CNN and YOLO (You Only Look Once) leading the way.

8.7 Image Classification

Image classification assigns labels or categories to images. CNNs are also widely used for image classification tasks and have achieved human-level performance in various domains.

8.8 Image Recognition Applications

Computer vision is applied in diverse fields, including:

Autonomous Vehicles: For recognizing pedestrians, other vehicles, and traffic signs.

Healthcare: In medical image analysis for diagnosis.

Agriculture: For crop monitoring and disease detection.

Augmented Reality: Enhancing real-world views with digital information.

8.9 Deep Learning in Computer Vision

Deep learning, particularly CNNs, has revolutionized computer vision. Models like VGG, ResNet, and Inception have achieved remarkable accuracy on image-related tasks.

8.10 Python Libraries for Computer Vision

Python offers powerful libraries for computer vision, including OpenCV for image processing and manipulation, and PyTorch and TensorFlow for deep learning-based vision tasks.

```
import tensorflow as tf
from tensorflow.keras.applications import ResNet50
from tensorflow.keras.applications.resnet50 import preprocess_input,
decode_predictions
from tensorflow.keras.preprocessing import image
import numpy as np

# Load the pre-trained ResNet model
model = ResNet50(weights='imagenet')

# Load and preprocess an image
img_path = 'path_to_image.jpg'
img = image.load_img(img_path, target_size=(224, 224))
img_array = image.img_to_array(img)
img_array = np.expand_dims(img_array, axis=0)
img_array = preprocess_input(img_array)

# Make predictions
predictions = model.predict(img_array)
decoded_predictions = decode_predictions(predictions, top=3)[0]

# Print the top 3 predicted classes and their probabilities
for class_id, class_label, probability in decoded_predictions:
    print(f"{class_label}: {probability:.2f}")
```

8.11 Example: Image Classification with TensorFlow and Keras

Here's an example of image classification using TensorFlow and Keras with a pre-trained ResNet model:

In this code, we use a pre-trained ResNet50 model to classify an image.

Computer Vision is at the forefront of AI and has far-reaching applications, from improving healthcare to enhancing entertainment experiences. Understanding computer vision principles and tools is essential for developing innovative solutions in this field.

Chapter 9: Natural Language Generation

9.1 Introduction to Natural Language Generation (NLG)

Natural Language Generation is the AI-driven process of generating human-like text or speech from structured data or other forms of non-linguistic input. NLG has applications in chatbots, content generation, data reporting, and more.

9.2 Data-to-Text Generation

Data-to-text generation involves transforming structured data, such as databases or spreadsheets, into natural language text. This is useful for generating reports, product descriptions, and personalized messages.

9.3 Rule-Based NLG

Rule-based NLG systems rely on predefined templates and rules to generate text. They are often used in scenarios where content structure is consistent.

9.4 Template-Based NLG

Template-based NLG systems use predefined templates that can be filled in with variable data. These templates allow for flexibility while maintaining consistency.

9.5 Data-Driven NLG

Data-driven NLG systems learn from data to generate text. They use techniques like regression models or neural networks to map data to language.

9.6 Content Planning

Content planning involves deciding what information to include in generated text. It often relies on domain-specific knowledge and preferences.

9.7 Surface Realization

Surface realization is the process of converting abstract content into grammatically correct and coherent language. It involves tasks like sentence structuring and language generation.

9.8 Text Summarization

Text summarization is a form of NLG that condenses longer texts into shorter, coherent summaries. It's used in news aggregation, document summarization, and more.

9.9 Chatbots and Virtual Assistants

Chatbots and virtual assistants use NLG to provide human-like responses in natural language. They are deployed in customer support, virtual shopping assistants, and more.

9.10 Multimodal NLG

Multimodal NLG combines text generation with other modalities like images or videos to create rich content experiences.

9.11 Python Libraries for NLG

```python
import openai
# Set your API key
api_key = 'YOUR_API_KEY'

# Initialize the GPT-3 client
openai.api_key = api_key

# Generate text using GPT-3
response = openai.Completion.create(
    engine="text-davinci-002",
    prompt="Translate the following English text to French: 'Hello, how
are you?'",
    max_tokens=50,
)
generated_text = response.choices[0].text
print("Generated Text:" generated text)
```

Python libraries like NLTK, spaCy, GPT-3 (via OpenAI's API), and NLG-specific frameworks like SimpleNLG provide tools for NLG tasks.

9.12 Example: Text Generation with GPT-3

Here's an example of text generation using OpenAI's GPT-3 API:

In this code, we use the GPT-3 API to translate English text into French.

NLG is a powerful technology for generating human-like text from data, enabling automated content creation, personalized messaging, and more. Understanding NLG techniques and tools is valuable for content generation applications.

In the upcoming chapters, we'll delve into advanced AI and machine learning topics and their practical implementations.

Chapter 10: Reinforcement Learning in Robotics

10.1 Introduction to Reinforcement Learning in Robotics

Reinforcement Learning (RL) is a natural fit for robotics, as it enables agents to learn actions by interacting with the environment. In this chapter, we explore the application of RL in robotics.

10.2 Robot Control as an RL Problem

In RL, a robot's actions are determined by an agent, which receives feedback (rewards) from the environment. The goal is for the agent to learn a policy that maximizes cumulative rewards over time.

10.3 Challenges in Robotic RL

Robotic RL poses unique challenges, such as:

High-Dimensional State Spaces: Robots often have to deal with a large number of sensors and actuators.

Safety: Ensuring safe interactions with the physical world is critical.

Exploration: Balancing exploration and exploitation is challenging in the real world.

Continuous Action Spaces: Robots often require precise continuous control.

10.4 Robotic Simulators

To train RL agents in robotics, simulators are commonly used. These simulators replicate the robot's dynamics and allow for safe and efficient training.

10.5 Reinforcement Learning Algorithms for Robotics

Several RL algorithms are used in robotics, including Proximal Policy Optimization (PPO), Trust Region Policy Optimization (TRPO), and Deep Deterministic Policy Gradients (DDPG).

10.6 Applications of RL in Robotics

RL is applied in various robotic domains, including:

- Robot Arm Control: Teaching robotic arms to manipulate objects.
- Autonomous Vehicles: Training self-driving cars to navigate.
- Drone Control: Enabling drones to perform tasks like package delivery.
- Humanoid Robots: Teaching robots to walk and interact with the environment.

10.7 Challenges in Real-World Robotics

While RL has shown promise in simulation, transferring learned policies to real robots presents additional challenges, such as sensor noise and discrepancies between simulation and reality.

10.8 Example: Robot Arm Control with RL

Here's an example of training a robot arm to reach a target using RL:

This code outlines the general structure of training a robot arm using RL in a custom environment.

```
import gym
import numpy as np
import tensorflow as tf
from tensorflow.keras import layers

# Create a custom RL environment or use an existing one like OpenAI
Gym
env = gym.make('CustomRobotArm-v0')

# Define a neural network policy model
model = tf.keras.Sequential([
    layers.Dense(64, activation='relu',
input_shape=(env.observation_space.shape[0],)),
    layers.Dense(64, activation='relu'),
    layers.Dense(env.action_space.shape[0], activation='tanh')
])
# Define the RL algorithm (e.g., PPO) and train the model
# (RL algorithm implementation details not shown here)
# Use the trained model to control the robot arm in the real world
# (Real-world control and hardware interface details are application-
specific)
```

Reinforcement Learning in robotics is a cutting-edge field with the potential to revolutionize automation and autonomous systems. Understanding RL algorithms, simulators, and real-world challenges is essential for building intelligent robots.

In the following chapters, we'll explore advanced AI and machine learning topics and their practical applications.

Chapter 11: Explainable AI (XAI)

11.1 Introduction to Explainable AI (XAI)

Explainable AI (XAI) is a field of artificial intelligence that focuses on making machine learning models and their decisions more transparent and interpretable to humans. XAI is essential for building trust, understanding model behavior, and ensuring ethical AI applications.

11.2 The Need for XAI

As AI models become more complex and powerful, there's a growing need to understand why AI systems make certain decisions. This is crucial in applications like healthcare, finance, and autonomous vehicles.

11.3 Black-Box vs. White-Box Models

Black-box models, like deep neural networks, are challenging to interpret because they lack transparency. White-box models, such as decision trees or linear regression, are inherently interpretable.

11.4 Techniques for XAI

Several techniques and methods are used for XAI, including:

Feature Importance: Identifying which features or variables are most influential in a model's predictions.

LIME (Local Interpretable Model-agnostic Explanations): Generating locally faithful explanations for model predictions.

SHAP (SHapley Additive exPlanations): Assigning contributions of each feature to the model's output in a cooperative game-theoretic manner.

Rule-Based Models: Creating human-readable rules that mimic the behavior of complex models.

Attention Mechanisms: Visualizing attention weights in models like transformers to understand their decision-making process.

Counterfactual Explanations: Generating examples of inputs that would have resulted in different model predictions.

Model Distillation: Training a simpler, interpretable model to mimic the behavior of a complex model.

11.5 Tools for XAI

There are various tools and libraries for implementing XAI techniques, including SHAP, LIME, and interpretML, which provide Python-based interfaces for model interpretation.

11.6 Ethical Considerations

XAI plays a crucial role in ensuring fairness, accountability, and transparency in AI systems. It helps detect and mitigate biases and enables AI practitioners to make ethical decisions.

11.7 XAI in Real-World Applications

XAI is applied in diverse domains, including:

Healthcare: Interpreting medical diagnoses made by AI systems.

```
import shap
import xgboost

# Load the XGBoost model
model = xgboost.XGBClassifier()
model.load_model('model_file_path')

# Create a SHAP explainer
explainer = shap.Explainer(model)

# Explain a single prediction
sample = X_test[0]  # Replace with your test data
shap_values = explainer(sample)

# Visualize feature importance
shap.plots.waterfall(shap_values[0])
```

Finance: Explaining credit approval or denial decisions.

Autonomous Vehicles: Understanding the reasoning behind self-driving car actions.

Legal: Supporting legal cases involving AI-generated evidence.

11.8 Example: Visualizing Model Interpretability with SHAP

Here's an example of using the SHAP library to visualize feature importance for a machine learning model:

This code demonstrates how to use SHAP to explain the predictions of a machine learning model.

Explainable AI is crucial for AI adoption in critical applications and for building AI systems that are transparent, accountable, and trusted. Understanding XAI techniques and tools is essential for AI practitioners and researchers.

Chapter 12: Generative Adversarial Networks (GANs)

12.1 Introduction to Generative Adversarial Networks (GANs)

Generative Adversarial Networks (GANs) are a class of machine learning models designed for generating synthetic data that closely resembles real data. GANs consist of two neural networks, a generator, and a discriminator, which are trained in a competitive process.

12.2 How GANs Work

Generator: The generator network takes random noise as input and generates data samples that aim to mimic real data.

Discriminator: The discriminator network evaluates whether a given data sample is real (from the training dataset) or fake (generated by the generator).

Training Process: GANs are trained through a min-max game. The generator aims to produce data that fools the discriminator, while the discriminator strives to become better at distinguishing real from fake data.

12.3 GAN Architectures

There are various GAN architectures designed for different tasks, including:

Vanilla GANs: The original GAN architecture.

DCGAN (Deep Convolutional GANs): GANs with deep convolutional neural networks, suitable for image generation.

Conditional GANs: GANs that generate data conditioned on specific input information.

CycleGAN: GANs for image-to-image translation tasks.

StyleGAN: GANs that enable control over the style and attributes of generated images.

12.4 Applications of GANs

GANs have a wide range of applications, such as:

- Image Generation: Creating realistic images of faces, animals, or scenes.
- Style Transfer: Transforming the style of images.
- Super-Resolution: Enhancing image resolution.
- Data Augmentation: Generating synthetic data to improve model performance.

- Art and Creativity: Generating art and music.
- Anonymization: Protecting privacy by generating synthetic data.

12.5 Ethical Considerations

GANs raise ethical concerns, especially when used for generating deepfake content, misinformation, or unauthorized data synthesis. Ensuring responsible use of GANs is essential.

12.6 Example: Image Generation with StyleGAN2

Here's an example of using StyleGAN2 to generate realistic faces:

This code demonstrates how to use StyleGAN2 to generate a face image from random noise.

Generative Adversarial Networks are a powerful tool

```
import dnnlib

import dnnlib.tflib as tflib


# Load the pre-trained StyleGAN2 model

tflib.init_tf()

url = 'https://nvlabs-fi-cdn.nvidia.com/stylegan2-ada/pretrained/ffhq.pkl'

with dnnlib.util.open_url(url) as f:

    generator_network, discriminator_network, Gs = pickle.load(f)

# Generate an image

z = np.random.randn(1, Gs.input_shape[1])  # Random noise vector

images = Gs.run(z, None, truncation_psi=0.7, randomize_noise=False,
output_transform=dict(func=tflib.convert_images_to_uint8))

PIL.Image.fromarray(images[0], 'RGB')
```

for data generation and creative applications. Understanding GAN architectures and responsible use is essential for leveraging their potential while addressing ethical concerns.

Chapter 13: Federated Learning

13.1 Introduction to Federated Learning

Federated Learning is a decentralized machine learning approach that enables model training across multiple devices or edge devices while keeping data localized and private. It addresses privacy concerns and is well-suited for scenarios with distributed data sources.

13.2 The Traditional Machine Learning Paradigm

In traditional machine learning, data is centralized, and model training occurs on a centralized server or cloud. This approach raises privacy and security concerns, especially when sensitive data is involved.

13.3 Federated Learning Workflow

The Federated Learning process involves the following steps:

Initialization: A global model is initialized on a central server.

Device Training: Local devices (e.g., smartphones) download the global model, improve it using their local data, and send model updates back to the server.

Aggregation: The server aggregates the model updates from multiple devices to create an improved global model.

Iteration: The process repeats iteratively, with devices continuously improving the global model while keeping data local.

13.4 Privacy and Security in Federated Learning

Federated Learning offers several privacy and security advantages:

Data Privacy: Raw data stays on local devices, reducing the risk of data breaches.

Differential Privacy: Techniques like differential privacy can be incorporated to further protect data.

Model Privacy: Federated Averaging helps protect the model's privacy by aggregating noisy updates.

13.5 Applications of Federated Learning

Federated Learning is applied in various domains, including:

- Healthcare: Collaborative model training for medical research while preserving patient data privacy.
- Mobile Devices: Improving predictive text, autocomplete, and recommendation systems.
- Internet of Things (IoT): Edge devices collaboratively training models for local decision-making.
- Financial Services: Collaborative fraud detection without sharing sensitive transaction data.

13.6 Federated Learning Frameworks

Several federated learning frameworks are available, including TensorFlow Federated (TFF) and PySyft, which provide tools and APIs for building federated learning systems.

13.7 Federated Learning in Practice

Implementing Federated Learning requires expertise in setting up a federated server, managing client devices, and handling communication protocols. Libraries and frameworks simplify the process.

13.8 Example: Federated Learning with TensorFlow Federated (TFF)

Here's a simplified example of federated learning using TensorFlow Federated (TFF):

This code outlines the structure of a federated learning process using TensorFlow Federated (TFF).

Federated Learning is a promising approach for training machine learning models in a privacy-preserving manner across distributed devices. Understanding the principles and tools of federated learning is essential for addressing privacy concerns in modern AI applications.

Chapter 14: Quantum Machine Learning

14.1 Introduction to Quantum Machine Learning

Quantum Machine Learning (QML) is an interdisciplinary field that explores the synergy between quantum computing and machine learning. It leverages quantum computing's unique properties to potentially solve complex problems faster and more efficiently.

14.2 Quantum Computing Basics

Quantum computers use qubits as their fundamental units, which can exist in superposition and entanglement states. Quantum algorithms can perform certain computations exponentially faster than classical computers, which opens new possibilities for machine learning.

14.3 Quantum Machine Learning Algorithms

Several quantum algorithms have been proposed for machine learning tasks, including:

- Quantum Support Vector Machines (QSVM): A quantum analog of classical SVM for classification tasks.
- Quantum Variational Circuits: Parameterized quantum circuits used for optimization tasks.
- Quantum Boltzmann Machines: Quantum versions of classical Boltzmann machines for probabilistic modeling.

14.4 Quantum Machine Learning Frameworks

Frameworks like Qiskit and Cirq provide tools for developing quantum machine learning algorithms and running them on quantum hardware or simulators.

14.5 Hybrid Quantum-Classical Machine Learning

Most practical QML approaches involve hybrid quantum-classical models. Classical computers handle preprocessing, optimization, and post-processing, while quantum computers perform specific quantum tasks.

14.6 Applications of Quantum Machine Learning

QML has the potential to impact various fields, including:

Drug Discovery: Speeding up molecular simulations and drug candidate screening.

Optimization: Solving complex optimization problems faster.

Cryptography: Enhancing security through quantum-resistant algorithms.

Machine Learning Acceleration: Speeding up training and inference for classical ML models.

14.7 Challenges and Limitations

QML faces challenges such as error rates in quantum hardware, the need for error correction, and the limited availability of quantum devices.

14.8 Example: Quantum Variational Circuit for Optimization

Here's a simplified example of using a quantum

```python
import numpy as np
from qiskit import QuantumCircuit, Aer, transpile
from qiskit.visualization import plot_bloch_multivector
from qiskit.aqua.algorithms import VQE,
NumPyMinimumEigensolver
from qiskit.circuit.library import TwoLocal
from qiskit.algorithms.optimizers import COBYLA

# Create a quantum circuit
qc = QuantumCircuit(3, 3)
qc.h(0)
qc.cx(0, 1)
qc.cx(1, 2)
qc.measure([0, 1, 2], [0, 1, 2])

# Visualize the quantum circuit
qc.draw()

# Simulate the quantum circuit
backend = Aer.get_backend('qasm_simulator')
compiled_circuit = transpile(qc, backend)
job = backend.run(compiled_circuit, shots=1024)
result = job.result()
counts = result.get_counts(qc)
print(counts)
```

variational circuit for optimization with Qiskit.

Quantum Machine Learning represents an exciting frontier in AI and has the potential to revolutionize various industries. While QML is still in its early stages, understanding its principles and tools is essential for staying at the forefront of AI research and development.

Chapter 15: AI Ethics and Responsible AI

15.1 Introduction to AI Ethics

AI Ethics refers to the moral and societal considerations surrounding the development and deployment of artificial intelligence technologies. It addresses issues of fairness, transparency, accountability, bias, and the impact of AI on individuals and society.

15.2 Fairness in AI

Fairness in AI aims to prevent discrimination and bias in algorithmic decision-making. Techniques like fairness-aware machine learning and bias detection are used to identify and mitigate bias in AI systems.

15.3 Transparency and Explainability

Explainability in AI involves making the decisions of machine learning models understandable to humans. It is essential for building trust and ensuring accountability. Methods such as LIME and SHAP help explain black-box models.

15.4 Accountability and Responsibility

AI systems should be designed with clear lines of responsibility. Developers, organizations, and regulators should be accountable for the consequences of AI system behavior.

15.5 Data Privacy

AI systems often rely on large datasets, raising concerns about data privacy. Privacy-preserving techniques like federated learning and differential privacy help protect sensitive data.

15.6 Ethical Considerations

AI ethics includes addressing questions about the ethical use of AI in various domains, such as healthcare, finance, and criminal justice. It also involves considering the potential misuse of AI.

15.7 Regulations and Standards

Governments and organizations are developing regulations and ethical frameworks for AI. GDPR in

Europe and AI ethics guidelines from organizations like IEEE and ACM are examples of such efforts.

15.8 Responsible AI Practices

Developers and organizations should adopt responsible AI practices, including:

- Data Governance: Ensuring ethical data collection, handling, and storage.
- Model Validation: Regularly assessing and validating model performance and fairness.
- Bias Mitigation: Implementing strategies to reduce bias in training data and models.
- Consent: Obtaining informed consent when using personal data.
- Impact Assessment: Evaluating the societal impact of AI applications.

15.9 AI Ethics Committees

Many organizations have established AI ethics committees or advisory boards to provide guidance and oversight in ethical AI development.

15.10 Example: Fairness Assessment of a Loan Approval Model

Here's an example of assessing fairness in a loan approval model:

- Data Collection: Collect historical loan application data, including applicant demographics and loan outcomes.

- Preprocessing: Analyze the data for potential bias based on gender, race, or other sensitive attributes.

- Bias Mitigation: Use techniques like re-sampling or re-weighting to reduce bias in the dataset.

- Model Training: Train a loan approval model using fairness-aware machine learning algorithms.

- Fairness Evaluation: Evaluate the model's fairness using metrics like disparate impact and equal opportunity.

- Continuous Monitoring: Continuously monitor the model's performance for fairness and update as needed.

AI ethics and responsible AI practices are essential for ensuring that AI technologies benefit society without causing harm or discrimination. Understanding these principles is crucial for AI developers, organizations, and policymakers.

Chapter 16: AI in Healthcare

16.1 Introduction to AI in Healthcare

AI is making significant contributions to healthcare by enhancing diagnosis, treatment, and patient care. It leverages medical data and advanced algorithms to improve healthcare outcomes.

16.2 Medical Imaging and Diagnosis

AI is used in medical imaging to aid in the detection and diagnosis of diseases such as cancer, pneumonia, and diabetic retinopathy. Deep learning models analyze medical images like X-rays, MRIs, and CT scans to identify abnormalities.

16.3 Drug Discovery and Development

AI accelerates drug discovery by predicting potential drug candidates, analyzing molecular interactions, and optimizing clinical trial designs. It reduces the time and cost of bringing new drugs to market.

16.4 Electronic Health Records (EHR)

AI assists in managing and extracting insights from electronic health records (EHRs). Natural language processing (NLP) is used to extract valuable information from unstructured clinical notes.

16.5 Personalized Medicine

AI tailors treatment plans to individual patients based on their genetic makeup, medical history, and specific health conditions. It helps identify the most effective treatments and medications.

16.6 Telemedicine and Remote Monitoring

AI enables remote healthcare delivery and patient monitoring through telemedicine platforms and wearable devices. It provides timely healthcare access, especially in remote areas.

16.7 Predictive Analytics

Machine learning models predict disease outbreaks, patient readmissions, and disease progression. This information helps healthcare providers allocate resources effectively.

16.8 AI in Surgery

Robotic surgical systems and AI-assisted surgery enhance the precision and efficiency of surgical procedures. Surgeons can perform minimally invasive surgeries with greater accuracy.

16.9 Ethical Considerations in AI Healthcare

AI in healthcare raises ethical concerns related to patient privacy, data security, bias in algorithms, and the need for human oversight in critical decisions.

16.10 Regulatory Compliance

Healthcare AI systems must comply with regulations like HIPAA in the United States and GDPR in Europe to protect patient data and privacy.

16.11 Example: AI in Medical Imaging

Here's an example of AI in medical imaging for detecting diabetic retinopathy using a deep learning model:

- Data Collection: Gather a large dataset of retinal images with corresponding disease labels.

- Preprocessing: Normalize and augment the image data to improve model training.

- Model Training: Train a convolutional neural network (CNN) on the dataset to classify images into different disease severity levels.

- Evaluation: Assess the model's performance using metrics like accuracy, sensitivity, and specificity.

- Clinical Integration: Deploy the trained model in a clinical setting to assist ophthalmologists in diagnosing diabetic retinopathy.

AI is revolutionizing healthcare by improving diagnosis, treatment, and patient care. Understanding AI applications in healthcare and the associated ethical and regulatory considerations is vital for healthcare professionals and AI developers.

Chapter 17: AI in Finance

17.1 Introduction to AI in Finance

Artificial intelligence has a profound impact on the financial industry by enhancing decision-making, risk management, fraud detection, and customer service. AI-driven algorithms analyze vast datasets and deliver insights at unprecedented speed.

17.2 Algorithmic Trading

AI-powered trading algorithms execute buy and sell orders in financial markets. Machine learning models analyze market data, news sentiment, and historical patterns to make trading decisions.

17.3 Risk Assessment and Management

AI assesses financial risk by analyzing customer data, credit scores, and market conditions. It helps financial institutions make informed lending decisions and manage portfolio risk.

17.4 Fraud Detection

AI detects fraudulent transactions by analyzing transaction data, behavior, and historical fraud patterns. It enhances security by identifying and preventing fraudulent activities.

17.5 Customer Service and Chatbots

AI-driven chatbots provide customer support, answer inquiries, and assist with account management. They offer 24/7 availability and improve customer satisfaction.

17.6 Wealth Management and Personal Finance

AI-powered robo-advisors offer investment advice and portfolio management based on individual financial goals and risk tolerance. They provide cost-effective investment solutions.

17.7 Regulatory Compliance

AI helps financial institutions comply with regulations by automating tasks like anti-money laundering (AML) and know your customer (KYC) checks. It reduces compliance costs and errors.

17.8 Credit Scoring

AI analyzes credit history and alternative data sources to assess an individual's creditworthiness. It expands access to credit for individuals with limited credit history.

17.9 Ethical Considerations in AI Finance

AI in finance raises ethical concerns related to fairness in lending, algorithmic bias, transparency in decision-making, and data privacy. Regulations like GDPR and consumer protection laws address these concerns.

17.10 Regulatory Compliance

Financial institutions must comply with regulations such as Dodd-Frank, Basel III, and MiFID II when implementing AI solutions. Regulatory compliance ensures financial stability and consumer protection.

17.11 Example: Algorithmic Trading

Here's an example of AI-powered algorithmic trading using a machine learning model:

- Data Collection: Gather historical market data, including price, volume, and news sentiment.

- Feature Engineering: Create relevant features from the raw data, such as moving averages, volatility, and technical indicators.

- Model Training: Train a machine learning model, such as a recurrent neural network (RNN) or a gradient boosting machine (GBM), to predict future price movements.

- Strategy Implementation: Implement the trading strategy based on the model's predictions, including buy/sell signals and risk management rules.

- Backtesting: Evaluate the strategy's performance using historical data to assess its profitability and risk.

AI is transforming the financial industry by automating tasks, improving decision-making, and enhancing customer experiences. Understanding AI applications in finance and their regulatory implications is essential for finance professionals and AI developers.

Chapter 18: AI in Natural Language Processing

18.1 Introduction to AI in Natural Language Processing (NLP)

Natural Language Processing is a subfield of AI that focuses on the interaction between humans and computers through natural language. AI-powered NLP systems process, understand, and generate human language.

18.2 Language Understanding

AI models, such as transformers, are used for language understanding tasks, including:

Sentiment Analysis: Determining the sentiment or emotion expressed in text.

Named Entity Recognition (NER): Identifying entities like names, dates, and locations in text.

Part-of-Speech Tagging: Assigning grammatical tags to words in sentences.

18.3 Machine Translation
AI-driven machine translation systems like Google Translate and neural machine translation models can translate text between languages with high accuracy.

18.4 Text Generation
Text generation models, such as GPT-3, can generate human-like text for various applications, including content creation, chatbots, and creative writing.

18.5 Question-Answering Systems
AI-based question-answering systems can extract answers from text documents or provide answers based on knowledge graphs.

18.6 Chatbots and Virtual Assistants
AI chatbots and virtual assistants interact with s in natural language. They are used in customer support, information retrieval, and task automation.

18.7 Sentiment Analysis in Social Media

AI analyzes social media content to understand public sentiment, track trends, and detect emerging issues.

18.8 Multilingual NLP

AI systems are developed to process and understand multiple languages, enabling global applications.

18.9 Ethical Considerations in NLP

AI in NLP raises ethical concerns related to bias in language models, privacy in text data, and the potential for generating harmful content.

18.10 Responsible AI in NLP

Developers and organizations should implement responsible AI practices, including bias detection and mitigation, content moderation, and privacy protection.

```python
import nltk
from nltk.sentiment.vader import SentimentIntensityAnalyzer

# Initialize the sentiment analyzer
nltk.download('vader_lexicon')
sia = SentimentIntensityAnalyzer()

# Analyze sentiment
text = "I love this product! It's amazing."
sentiment = sia.polarity_scores(text)

# Interpret sentiment scores
if sentiment['compound'] >= 0.05:
    sentiment_label = "Positive"
elif sentiment['compound'] <= -0.05:
    sentiment_label = "Negative"
else:
    sentiment_label = "Neutral"

print("Sentiment:", sentiment_label)
```

18.11 Example: Sentiment Analysis with Python

Here's an example of performing sentiment analysis using Python and the Natural Language Toolkit (NLTK):

This code demonstrates how to perform sentiment analysis on text using NLTK's VADER sentiment analyzer.

AI in Natural Language Processing plays a crucial role in understanding and generating human language, enabling applications in communication, content analysis, and information retrieval. Understanding NLP techniques and ethical considerations is essential for AI developers and linguists.

Chapter 19: AI in Computer Vision

19.1 Introduction to AI in Computer Vision

Computer Vision is a field of artificial intelligence that focuses on teaching machines to interpret and understand visual information from the world, including images and videos. AI in computer vision has numerous applications across industries.

19.2 Image Classification

AI models classify images into predefined categories, such as identifying objects in photos. Convolutional Neural Networks (CNNs) are commonly used for image classification tasks.

19.3 Object Detection

Object detection algorithms locate and identify multiple objects within an image. They are used in applications like autonomous vehicles and surveillance systems.

19.4 Image Segmentation

Image segmentation divides an image into regions or segments based on similar characteristics. It's used in medical imaging, autonomous navigation, and video editing.

19.5 Face Recognition

AI-powered face recognition systems can identify and verify individuals from images or video frames. They have applications in security, authentication, and personalization.

19.6 Optical Character Recognition (OCR)

OCR technology converts printed or handwritten text from images into machine-readable text. It's used in document digitization and data extraction.

19.7 Pose Estimation

Pose estimation algorithms determine the pose or position of objects or body parts within an image or video. They are used in augmented reality and robotics.

19.8 Image Generation

Generative models like GANs can generate realistic images based on input data, enabling creative applications and content generation.

19.9 Autonomous Vehicles

Computer vision is crucial for autonomous vehicles, enabling them to perceive the environment, detect obstacles, and make driving decisions.

19.10 Medical Imaging

AI in medical imaging assists in diagnosing diseases, analyzing medical images, and planning treatments. It includes applications like X-ray interpretation and MRI analysis.

19.11 Ethical Considerations in Computer Vision

AI in computer vision raises ethical concerns related to privacy, surveillance, and bias in algorithms. Responsible AI practices are essential for addressing these concerns.

```
import tensorflow as tf
import cv2

# Load the pre-trained object detection model
model = tf.saved_model.load("path_to_saved_model")

# Load and preprocess an image
image = cv2.imread("image_path")
input_tensor = tf.convert_to_tensor(image)
input_tensor = input_tensor[tf.newaxis, ...]

# Perform object detection
detections = model(input_tensor)

# Process detection results (e.g., draw bounding boxes on
the image)
# ...

# Display the annotated image
cv2.imshow("Object Detection", image)
cv2.waitKey(0)
cv2.destroyAllWindows()
```

19.12 Responsible AI in Computer Vision

Developers should implement responsible AI practices, including data anonymization, transparency in AI decision-making, and fairness evaluations.

19.13 Example: Object Detection with Python and TensorFlow

Here's an example of object detection using Python and TensorFlow's Object Detection API:

This code outlines the process of performing object detection using a pre-trained TensorFlow model.

AI in computer vision has transformative applications across various domains, from healthcare to autonomous systems. Understanding computer vision techniques and their ethical implications is crucial for AI developers and researchers.

Chapter 20: Reinforcement Learning

20.1 Introduction to Reinforcement Learning

Reinforcement Learning (RL) is a branch of machine learning that focuses on training agents to make sequential decisions to maximize a cumulative reward. RL is widely used in applications like robotics, game playing, and autonomous systems.

20.2 Components of Reinforcement Learning

Agent: The learner or decision-maker that interacts with the environment.

Environment: The external system with which the agent interacts.

State (s): A representation of the environment at a given time.

Action (a): The choices made by the agent to interact with the environment.

Policy (π): The strategy or mapping from states to actions.

Reward (r): A scalar feedback signal indicating the immediate desirability of an action.

Value Function (V or Q): Estimates of expected cumulative rewards for states or state-action pairs.

20.3 Markov Decision Processes (MDPs)

MDPs are a mathematical framework used to model RL problems. They consist of states, actions, transition probabilities, rewards, and a discount factor.

20.4 Exploration vs. Exploitation

RL agents face the dilemma of balancing exploration (trying new actions to learn) and exploitation (choosing known actions for immediate rewards). Various strategies, such as epsilon-greedy policies, are used to address this trade-off.

20.5 Deep Reinforcement Learning

Deep Reinforcement Learning combines RL with deep neural networks. Algorithms like Deep Q-Networks

```python
import gym
import tensorflow as tf
import numpy as np

# Create the CartPole environment
env = gym.make('CartPole-v1')

# Define a neural network model for the agent
model = tf.keras.Sequential([
    tf.keras.layers.Dense(24, activation='relu', input_shape=(env.observation_space.shape[0],)),
    tf.keras.layers.Dense(24, activation='relu'),
    tf.keras.layers.Dense(env.action_space.n, activation='linear')
])

# Define the optimizer and loss function
optimizer = tf.keras.optimizers.Adam(learning_rate=0.001)
loss_fn = tf.keras.losses.mean_squared_error

# Training loop
for episode in range(1000):
    state = env.reset()
    episode_reward = 0

    while True:
        # Choose an action using epsilon-greedy policy
        epsilon = 0.1
        if np.random.rand() < epsilon:
            action = env.action_space.sample()
        else:
            q_values = model.predict(state.reshape(1, -1))
            action = np.argmax(q_values)

        next_state, reward, done, _ = env.step(action)

        # Compute the target Q-value
        target = reward + 0.99 * np.max(model.predict(next_state.reshape(1, -1)))

        # Train the model
        with tf.GradientTape() as tape:
            q_values = model(state.reshape(1, -1))
            loss = loss_fn(target, q_values[0, action])

        grads = tape.gradient(loss, model.trainable_variables)
        optimizer.apply_gradients(zip(grads, model.trainable_variables))

        episode_reward += reward
        state = next_state

        if done:
            break

    print(f"Episode {episode}: Total Reward: {episode_reward}")

# Evaluate the trained agent
# ...
```

(DQN) and Proximal Policy Optimization (PPO) leverage deep learning for complex tasks.

20.6 Applications of Reinforcement Learning

RL is applied in diverse fields, including:

Game Playing: AlphaGo's victory over human Go champions.

Robotics: Training robots to perform tasks in real-world environments.

Healthcare: Personalized treatment plans and drug discovery.

Autonomous Vehicles: Self-driving cars learn to navigate roads safely.

Finance: Portfolio optimization and trading strategies.

20.7 Challenges in Reinforcement Learning

RL faces challenges such as sample inefficiency, exploration in high-dimensional spaces, and the need for careful hyperparameter tuning.

20.8 Example: Training a CartPole Agent with OpenAI Gym

Here's an example of training a CartPole agent using the OpenAI Gym and TensorFlow:

This code demonstrates training a CartPole agent using RL techniques with TensorFlow.

Reinforcement Learning is a powerful approach for training agents to make sequential decisions in complex environments. Understanding RL concepts and algorithms is essential for AI researchers and practitioners working on sequential decision-making problems.

Chapter 21: Transfer Learning in Machine Learning

21.1 Introduction to Transfer Learning

Transfer Learning is a machine learning technique that leverages knowledge learned from one task to improve performance on a related but different task. It allows models to benefit from pre-trained knowledge and reduces the need for extensive training data.

21.2 Motivation for Transfer Learning

Transfer Learning addresses challenges like data scarcity and computational resources by enabling models to generalize from existing knowledge. It is widely used in various domains, including computer vision, natural language processing, and reinforcement learning.

21.3 Types of Transfer Learning

Inductive Transfer Learning: Knowledge from a source task is used to initialize a model for a target task.

Transductive Transfer Learning: Knowledge from a source task is used to adapt a model to a specific target instance or distribution.

21.4 Pre-trained Models

Pre-trained models are neural networks trained on large datasets for generic tasks like image classification or language modeling. They serve as starting points for transfer learning.

21.5 Fine-tuning

Fine-tuning involves taking a pre-trained model and training it on a target task with a smaller dataset. The model's lower layers are often frozen, while higher layers are adapted to the new task.

21.6 Domain Adaptation

Domain adaptation focuses on transferring knowledge from a source domain to a target domain, even when the distributions of data are different.

21.7 Applications of Transfer Learning

Transfer Learning is applied in various domains, including:

Image Classification: Using pre-trained models for different image recognition tasks.

Text Classification: Transferring knowledge from large text corpora to specific text classification tasks.

Speech Recognition: Adapting pre-trained speech models to new languages or accents.

Autonomous Robotics: Transferring knowledge between different robotic tasks.

21.8 Challenges in Transfer Learning

Challenges include selecting the right source task, dealing with domain shift, and avoiding negative transfer where transferred knowledge hurts performance.

21.9 Example: Fine-tuning a Pre-

```python
import tensorflow as tf
from transformers import BertTokenizer,
TFBertForSequenceClassification
from transformers import glue_convert_examples_to_features

# Load pre-trained BERT model and tokenizer
model_name = "bert-base-uncased"
tokenizer = BertTokenizer.from_pretrained(model_name)
model =
TFBertForSequenceClassification.from_pretrained(model_name)

# Load and preprocess data
train_data = load_and_preprocess_data(train_file)
train_features = glue_convert_examples_to_features(train_data,
tokenizer, max_length=128, task="mrpc")

# Fine-tuning
optimizer = tf.keras.optimizers.Adam(learning_rate=2e-5)
loss =
tf.keras.losses.SparseCategoricalCrossentropy(from_logits=True)
model.compile(optimizer=optimizer, loss=loss, metrics=['accuracy'])
model.fit(train_features.shuffle(100).batch(32), epochs=3)

# Evaluate on target task
test_data = load_and_preprocess_data(test_file)
test_features = glue_convert_examples_to_features(test_data,
tokenizer, max_length=128, task="mrpc")
results = model.evaluate(test_features.batch(32))
print("Test accuracy:", results[1])
```

trained Language Model

Here's an example of fine-tuning a pre-trained language model (e.g., BERT) for sentiment analysis:

This code demonstrates fine-tuning a pre-trained BERT model for sentiment analysis on a target dataset.

Transfer Learning is a valuable technique for improving the performance of machine learning models on various tasks. Understanding how to apply and adapt pre-trained models is essential for AI practitioners and researchers.

Chapter 23: AI in Natural Language Generation

23.1 Introduction to AI in Natural Language Generation (NLG)

Natural Language Generation is a branch of AI that focuses on generating human-like text or speech from structured data. NLG has applications in content generation, chatbots, and report generation.

23.2 NLG Approaches

There are two primary approaches to NLG:

Rule-based NLG: NLG systems use predefined rules and templates to generate text.

Machine Learning-based NLG: NLG models are trained on large datasets to generate text based on patterns and examples.

23.3 Text Generation Models

Text generation models include:

Recurrent Neural Networks (RNNs): Sequential models that generate text character by character.

Transformer Models: Attention-based models that generate text by attending to input sequences.

GPT (Generative Pre-trained Transformer): A family of models known for their text generation capabilities.

23.4 Applications of NLG

NLG is applied in various domains:

Content Generation: Automatically generating news articles, product descriptions, and social media posts.

Chatbots: Creating conversational agents that generate human-like responses.

Data-to-Text: Converting structured data (e.g., financial reports) into human-readable narratives.

Personalization: Customizing text content for individual s.

23.5 Ethical Considerations in NLG

NLG raises ethical concerns related to misinformation, bias in generated content, and the potential for misuse in generating fake news.

23.6 Use Cases

Let's explore two NLG use cases:

Use Case 1: E-commerce Product Descriptions

Input Data: Product attributes, specifications, and reviews.

NLG Model: Transformer-based model.

Output: Automatically generated product descriptions highlighting key features and reviews.

Use Case 2: Financial Report Generation

Input Data: Financial data, charts, and tables.

NLG Model: RNN-based model.

Output: Automatically generated financial reports summarizing key insights and trends.

23.7 Challenges in NLG

Challenges in NLG include maintaining coherence in

```
import openai
# Initialize the GPT-3 API key
api_key = "your_api_key"
openai.api_key = api_key
# Generate text with GPT-3
response = openai.Completion.create(
    engine="text-davinci-002",
    prompt="Once upon a time, in a land far, far away,",
    max_tokens=100
)
generated_text = response.choices[0].text
print(generated_text)
```

generated text, ensuring readability, and avoiding plagiarism.

23.8 Example: Text Generation with GPT-3

Here's an example of text generation using OpenAI's GPT-3:

This code demonstrates how to generate text using GPT-3, a powerful NLG model.

NLG plays a vital role in automating text generation tasks and creating personalized content. Understanding NLG techniques is essential for content creators and developers working on text generation applications.

Chapter 24: AI in Recommender Systems

24.1 Introduction to Recommender Systems

Recommender systems are AI applications that provide personalized recommendations to s based on their preferences and behavior. They are widely used in e-commerce, streaming platforms, and content recommendations.

24.2 Types of Recommender Systems

There are two primary types of recommender systems:

Collaborative Filtering: Recommends items based on the preferences and behavior of similar items.

Content-Based Filtering: Recommends items similar to those a has shown interest in.

24.3 Hybrid Recommender Systems

Hybrid recommender systems combine collaborative and content-based filtering to provide more accurate and diverse recommendations.

24.4 Matrix Factorization

Matrix factorization techniques, like Singular Value Decomposition (SVD) and Matrix Factorization with Stochastic Gradient Descent (MF-SGD), are used in collaborative filtering.

24.5 Collaborative Filtering Algorithms

Collaborative filtering algorithms include -based and item-based approaches, as well as matrix factorization.

24.6 Content-Based Filtering

Content-based filtering recommends items by analyzing their attributes and matching them to a 's profile.

24.7 Neural Collaborative Filtering

Deep learning models, such as neural collaborative filtering (NeuCF), improve recommendation accuracy by capturing complex -item interactions.

24.8 Evaluating Recommender Systems

Common evaluation metrics for recommender systems include Mean Absolute Error (MAE), Root Mean Square Error (RMSE), and Precision at K.

24.9 Personalization and Profiling

Personalization is a key aspect of recommender systems, tailoring recommendations to individual s. profiling involves capturing preferences and behavior.

24.10 Ethical Considerations in Recommender Systems

Recommender systems raise ethical concerns, such as filter bubbles, echo chambers, and the potential for amplifying biases.

24.11 Use Case: Movie Recommendation System

Let's explore a movie recommendation system use case:

```python
from surprise import Dataset, Reader, SVD
from surprise.model_selection import train_test_split
from surprise import accuracy

# Load data
reader = Reader(rating_scale=(1, 5))
data = Dataset.load_builtin('ml-100k')
trainset, testset = train_test_split(data, test_size=0.25)

# Build and train the SVD model
model = SVD()
model.fit(trainset)

# Make predictions
predictions = model.test(testset)

# Evaluate the model
rmse = accuracy.rmse(predictions)
mae = accuracy.mae(predictions)

print(f"RMSE: {rmse:.2f}")
print(f"MAE: {mae:.2f}")
```

Collaborative Filtering: Recommends movies based on ratings and similarity to others.

Content-Based Filtering: Recommends movies based on genre, director, and actors.

Hybrid Approach: Combines collaborative and content-based filtering for personalized recommendations.

24.12 Challenges in Recommender Systems

Challenges include cold-start problems for new s or items, scalability, and privacy concerns.

24.13 Example: Building a Collaborative Filtering Recommender

Here's an example of building a collaborative filtering movie recommender using Python and the Surprise library:

This code demonstrates building a collaborative filtering recommender using the Surprise library and evaluating its performance.

Recommender systems play a vital role in enhancing experiences and driving engagement in various online platforms. Understanding recommender system techniques is essential for data scientists and developers working on recommendation applications.

Chapter 25: AI in Robotics

25.1 Introduction to AI in Robotics

Artificial Intelligence plays a pivotal role in robotics, enabling machines to perceive, reason, plan, and act autonomously in dynamic environments. Robotics combines AI with mechanical engineering and computer science to create intelligent machines.

25.2 Perception in Robotics

Perception involves sensors and algorithms that allow robots to understand their surroundings. Technologies like computer vision, LiDAR, and radar enable robots to recognize objects and navigate environments.

25.3 Planning and Decision-Making

AI-driven planning algorithms enable robots to determine the best actions to achieve their goals while considering obstacles and constraints.

25.4 Localization and Mapping (SLAM)

Simultaneous Localization and Mapping (SLAM) techniques help robots navigate unknown environments by building maps and estimating their own positions.

25.5 Control and Actuation

Control systems execute robot actions, translating high-level plans into motor commands. These systems ensure precise and safe movements.

25.6 Robot Learning

Machine learning, including reinforcement learning and imitation learning, allows robots to acquire new skills and adapt to changing conditions.

25.7 Robot Autonomy Levels

Robots can operate at various autonomy levels, from fully manual (teleoperated) to fully autonomous (capable of making decisions independently).

25.8 Robotic Applications

Robotics has diverse applications:

Industrial Robots: Used in manufacturing and logistics for tasks like welding, painting, and pick-and-place operations.

Autonomous Vehicles: Self-driving cars and drones leverage AI for navigation and control.

Healthcare Robots: Assistive robots aid patients and healthcare professionals in hospitals and care facilities.

Search and Rescue Robots: Deployed in disaster-stricken areas to locate survivors and assess damage.

25.9 Challenges in Robotics

Challenges include robustness in dynamic environments, human-robot interaction, and ethical considerations surrounding AI-powered robots.

25.10 Example: Autonomous Drone Navigation

Here's an example of autonomous drone navigation using AI:

- Sensors: The drone uses cameras and LiDAR to perceive its surroundings.
- Perception: Computer vision algorithms identify obstacles and terrain features.
- Planning: AI-based path planning algorithms calculate the optimal flight path.
- Control: Motor control systems adjust propeller speeds for stable flight.

25.11 Future Directions in Robotics

The future of robotics involves enhanced autonomy, human-robot collaboration, and the integration of AI with the Internet of Things (IoT).

25.12 Ethical Considerations in Robotics

Robots, especially those with AI capabilities, raise ethical concerns related to safety, privacy, job displacement, and accountability.

AI-driven robotics has the potential to revolutionize industries and improve our daily lives. Understanding the principles of AI in robotics is essential for engineers, researchers, and anyone interested in the future of automation.

Chapter 26: AI in Natural Language Understanding (NLU)

26.1 Introduction to AI in Natural Language Understanding (NLU)

Natural Language Understanding (NLU) is a subfield of Natural Language Processing (NLP) that focuses on enabling machines to comprehend and interpret human language in a meaningful way. NLU is essential for tasks such as question answering, sentiment analysis, and chatbots.

26.2 NLU vs. NLP

While NLP deals with a wide range of language-related tasks, NLU goes a step further by aiming to extract meaning and context from text or speech.

26.3 Key Components of NLU

NLU involves several key components:

- Tokenization: Breaking text into individual words or tokens.
- Syntax Analysis: Parsing sentences to understand grammatical structure.

- Semantic Analysis: Extracting the meaning and intent behind text.
- Discourse Analysis: Understanding context and connections between sentences.

26.4 Named Entity Recognition (NER)

NER is an NLU task that involves identifying and classifying entities in text, such as names, dates, locations, and organizations.

26.5 Intent Recognition

Intent recognition is crucial in chatbots and virtual assistants, as it involves determining a 's purpose or request from their input.

26.6 Question Answering Systems

NLU powers question answering systems that can extract answers from textual data, documents, or databases.

26.7 Sentiment Analysis

Sentiment analysis determines the emotional tone or sentiment expressed in text, such as positive, negative, or neutral.

26.8 Chatbots and Virtual Assistants

NLU enables chatbots and virtual assistants to understand queries and provide appropriate responses.

26.9 Ethical Considerations in NLU

Ethical concerns in NLU include privacy issues, responsible AI use, and addressing bias in language models.

26.10 Use Case: Intent Recognition for Chatbots

Let's explore an intent recognition use case for a chatbot:

Task: Recognizing intents in customer support chat interactions.

AI Model: A machine learning or deep learning model trained on labeled chat data.

```
import spacy

# Load spaCy NLP model

nlp = spacy.load("en_core_web_sm")


# Process text

text = "Apple Inc. is headquartered in
Cupertino, California. It was founded
by Steve Jobs."

doc = nlp(text)


# Extract named entities

entities = [(ent.text, ent.label_) for ent
in doc.ents]

print("Named Entities:", entities)
```

Application: Routing customer inquiries to the appropriate support team based on their intents.

26.11 Challenges in NLU

Challenges include handling ambiguity in language, context awareness, and the need for large and diverse training data.

26.12 Example: Named Entity Recognition (NER)

Here's an example of Named Entity Recognition (NER) using the spaCy library in Python:

This code demonstrates NER using spaCy to extract named entities and their labels from text.

NLU is essential for building intelligent systems that can understand and interact with humans in natural language. Understanding NLU techniques is valuable for developers, data scientists, and those working on conversational AI.

Chapter 27: AI in Autonomous Agents

27.1 Introduction to Autonomous Agents

Autonomous agents are intelligent entities that can perceive their environment, make decisions, and take actions to achieve specific goals. These agents are used in robotics, autonomous vehicles, game characters, and more. They rely on AI and machine learning to navigate and interact with their surroundings.

27.2 Perception in Autonomous Agents

Perception involves sensors and data processing to understand the environment. Common sensors include cameras, LiDAR, radar, and microphones. AI techniques, such as computer vision and sensor fusion, help agents interpret sensory data.

27.3 Decision-Making in Autonomous Agents

Decision-making algorithms enable agents to plan and choose actions. Reinforcement learning, Markov decision processes (MDPs), and planning algorithms play a significant role in autonomous decision-making.

27.4 Navigation and Path Planning

Navigation and path planning algorithms help agents find optimal routes to reach their destinations while avoiding obstacles. These algorithms are crucial in robotics and autonomous vehicles.

27.5 Simultaneous Localization and Mapping (SLAM)

SLAM is a technique used in robotics to create maps of an environment while simultaneously tracking the agent's location within that environment. SLAM enables agents to navigate unknown spaces.

27.6 Control Systems for Autonomous Agents

Control systems are responsible for executing actions and maintaining stability. Proportional-Integral-Derivative (PID) controllers and model predictive control (MPC) are commonly used in autonomous systems.

27.7 Machine Learning in Autonomous Agents

Machine learning, including deep reinforcement learning, helps agents adapt to dynamic environments and learn from experience. It enables agents to improve their decision-making and behavior over time.

27.8 Applications of Autonomous Agents

Autonomous agents find applications in various domains:

Robotics: Autonomous robots for tasks like cleaning, delivery, and exploration.

Autonomous Vehicles: Self-driving cars, drones, and unmanned aerial vehicles (UAVs).

Video Games: Non-player characters (NPCs) with realistic behavior and decision-making.

Healthcare: Autonomous surgical robots for minimally invasive procedures.

27.9 Ethical Considerations in Autonomous Agents

Ethical concerns include safety, liability, and ensuring that autonomous agents make ethical decisions in critical situations.

27.10 Use Case: Autonomous Drone Navigation

Let's explore an example of autonomous drone navigation:

Task: Autonomous drone delivery to a specified location.

AI Model: Combines computer vision for obstacle detection, path planning, and control systems.

Application: Efficient and safe drone delivery services.

27.11 Challenges in Autonomous Agents

Challenges include handling uncertainty in real-world environments, ensuring safety, and addressing ethical dilemmas.

27.12 Example: Simulating Autonomous Agents in a Virtual Environment

Here's an example of simulating autonomous agents in a virtual environment using Python and the Pygame library:

This code sets up a simple simulation of autonomous agents (blue circles) in a Pygame window.

```python
import pygame
import random

# Initialize Pygame
pygame.init()

# Create a window
window_size = (800, 600)
window = pygame.display.set_mode(window_size)
pygame.display.set_caption("Autonomous Agents Simulation")

# Define agent class
class Agent:
    def __init__(self):
        self.x = random.randint(0, window_size[0])
        self.y = random.randint(0, window_size[1])
        self.color = (0, 0, 255)  # Blue

    def move(self):
        # Implement agent movement logic here
        pass

    def draw(self):
        pygame.draw.circle(window, self.color, (self.x, self.y), 10)

# Create agents
num_agents = 5
agents = [Agent() for _ in range(num_agents)]

# Main loop
running = True
while running:
    for event in pygame.event.get():
        if event.type == pygame.QUIT:
            running = False

    # Move and draw agents
    for agent in agents:
        agent.move()
        agent.draw()

    pygame.display.flip()

# Quit Pygame
pygame.quit()
```

Autonomous agents are transforming industries and creating new possibilities for automation and intelligent decision-making. Understanding the principles of autonomous agents is valuable for robotics engineers, autonomous vehicle developers, and game developers.

Chapter 28: AI in Swarm Intelligence

28.1 Introduction to Swarm Intelligence

Swarm intelligence is inspired by the collective behavior of social animals like ants, bees, and birds. AI researchers use swarm intelligence algorithms to solve optimization and decision-making problems.

28.2 Swarm Algorithms

Swarm algorithms, such as Ant Colony Optimization (ACO) and Particle Swarm Optimization (PSO), simulate the interactions and behaviors of social organisms to find optimal solutions.

28.3 Applications of Swarm Intelligence

Swarm intelligence is applied in various domains:

Robotics: Coordinating groups of robots for tasks like search and rescue.

Logistics: Optimizing supply chain and transportation routes.

Finance: Portfolio optimization and trading strategies.

Internet of Things (IoT): Managing and routing data in IoT networks.

28.4 Challenges in Swarm Intelligence

Challenges include scalability, convergence speed, and adapting swarm algorithms to dynamic environments.

Chapter 29: AI in Biometrics

29.1 Introduction to Biometrics and AI

Biometrics involves using unique physical or behavioral characteristics for identification and authentication. AI is increasingly used to enhance biometric systems for security and convenience.

29.2 Biometric Modalities

Biometric systems can use various modalities, including fingerprints, facial recognition, iris scans, voice recognition, and gait analysis.

29.3 AI in Biometric Identification

AI algorithms, such as deep neural networks, improve the accuracy and robustness of biometric identification systems.

29.4 Applications of Biometrics

Biometric systems are used in:

Access Control: Unlocking devices or secure areas.

Banking: Secure mobile banking and transactions.

Law Enforcement: Criminal identification and forensic analysis.

Healthcare: Patient identification and access to medical records.

29.5 Ethical Considerations in Biometrics

Ethical concerns in biometrics include privacy, consent, and protecting biometric data from misuse.

Chapter 40: Conclusion

In this handbook on AI and ML, we've explored a wide range of topics, from fundamental concepts to advanced techniques and applications. AI and ML continue to transform industries and shape our future. Whether you're a student, researcher, developer, or business professional, understanding AI and ML is essential in today's data-driven world.

As technology evolves, it's crucial to stay updated with the latest developments, ethical considerations, and practical implementations of AI and ML. Keep exploring, learning, and innovating, and contribute to the exciting field of artificial intelligence.

Thank you for embarking on this journey through the Handbook to AI and ML.

www.ingramcontent.com/pod-product-compliance
Lightning Source LLC
Chambersburg PA
CBHW072211290526
45794CB00004B/1725